Leading With Compassion

A Guide to Successful Leadership by Building Trust and Gaining Commitment

Katherine Parks

Leading With Compassion

First Edition:

Copyright © 2011 Realeaders

All rights reserved.

Stockton, CA

ISBN: 0615458513
ISBN-13: 9780615458519
LCCN: 2011929841

Thank You

To my husband, Gerald: my hero whose laugh is contagious and strength is unending. I love you. You own my heart.

To my children, Katherine, Carol, Jerry, Vicki, Brian, and Elizabeth who give me the strength and courage to make every day count.

To my mom and brothers who taught me the meaning of unconditional love.

To Carri, Christina, Hope, Sue, Shelli, Toni and Ronda whose friendship is my greatest gift.

To all of the wonderful people I have worked with over the years who are the reason I love to be a leader.

Contents

Introduction: What is Compassion?

Chapter 1 ...Love in the Workplace

Chapter 2 ...Show Sympathy, be Empathetic

Chapter 3...Emotional Stability

Chapter 4 ...A Little Kindness Goes a Long Way

Conclusion... Compassion Breeds Commitment

Introduction: What is Compassion?

In today's world, compassion in leadership is an imperative. It's a must. As companies downsize or slow down growth to survive in this economy, more responsibilities are added to the already overfull plates of the people leaders. People need to know that their leader is there for them, even if "special projects" may take them away from their normal day-to-day people responsibilities. The best way to accomplish this is by leading with compassion. It is through compassion that we connect with one another.

My husband and I teach our four youngest children at home. To help increase their vocabulary, we give them a "word of the day" to define, spell and use in a sentence. I gave the word compassion to our 10-year-old daughter Vicki. She looked it up in the dictionary and then, to better understand how to use it in a sentence, did a search on the internet. Daunted by the many references the search gave her, she asked me to take a look.

The search results included the words love, sympathy, empathy, emotional maturity and kindness. Images included people holding hands, women holding babies, people holding each other, and people caring for the sick and elderly.

Throughout my twenty-five years in leadership roles, I built many successful teams. Because I sincerely cared for each member of every team, I manifested all these elements toward them. I told them how important they were to the company, and to me. It isn't difficult to display sympathy, empathy, emotional maturity and kindness -- compassion -- if that's in your nature. But the pressurized maelstrom of business culture can stamp these qualities out of one's nature and leave resentment and anxiety. Compassion bonds a leader to the team, whereas the lack of compassion separates them.

After helping Vicki research her word of the day I recognized that compassion is the most crucial component in good leadership. I also had the title to this book, which is chock-full of my experience. I will share with you the tools and skills that proved effective over the years, and all imbrued with the overarching motif of compassion.

I would rather feel compassion than know the meaning of it ~ Thomas Aquinas

Chapter 1

Love in the Workplace

Love is a strong connection between people that can promote admiration and dedication.

As the leader of a team, you want *dedicated* employees who *admire* your work ethic and leadership style. Love is a key ingredient in the recipe for building a successful team.

How else does love pay off in the workplace?

Leading With Compassion

Love is consistently associated with trust and patience. By showing patience and being trustworthy you demonstrate love, and the payoff comes when your team reciprocates. You will have a group of people who are dedicated. Can you handle that?

Trustworthiness

Many years ago I first heard the phrase "open door policy" and loved it. How great that the leader, the boss, the head honcho will welcome me into his office and listen to my thoughts, concerns, and maybe my gripes and peeves. The open-door promise is hard to fulfill. I have been told "I'm too busy," or had a bad boss ignore me and work on the computer as I spoke. But good bosses have welcomed me and listened attentively. They at least appeared to take me seriously.

When I became a leader I learned how hard it is to have an open-door policy. The people want to take you at your word. They walk through that open door, a lot. If people like and trust you they will bring their problems to you and expect help. Your open-door policy promises no less than a warm greeting and your rapt attention as well as help toward a solution. If you cannot offer these things, if you tell him to take it to someone else, or catch me later, that's not my area, or some such yada yada, then you need to change that open-door policy to a don't bug me, I'm busy policy.

It is so easy to backslide and cut the poor employee short shrift. You may be raging against a deadline. There may be secret assailants in the company working together to undercut you and get you fired. Paranoia may grip you like a baby grips your earring, but compassion will prevent you from hissing at your employee for climbing your last nerve.

I myself have erred in my illustrious career. While I always told my people I'm there for them, no matter what, I have failed that promise. One time I was overextended on projects and felt the cold grip of failure closing on my nape. One of my reps -- let's call her Penny -- breezed through my open door one afternoon. I remained fixated zombie-like on my computer. "Go ahead and talk," I told her, "I can split my concentration." It didn't occur to me as I banged away at the keyboard, that I had just stumbled down the slick slope of bad leadership. But Penny recognized it.

Still, she gave it a shot. As she talked, her words seemed like the grownups' voices in Charlie Brown cartoons. "Whaa whaaa whaaaaa," I heard, so I bobbed my head and mmmed and hmmed until her inflection changed. I gave her my hundred-watt smile and went for the closing. "Hey, that's really nice."

"Really nice?" Penny snapped. "Have you heard even one thing I've said?"

Oops. Penny's brother was very, very sick and she needed time off to care for him. I had completely ignored her story. Lucky for me Penny had compassion herself. She accepted my apology and we carried on. This time I met her eyes and listened. I gave her sincere sympathy and help in getting some time off.

Sometimes a listener is all the employee needs. Even if the problem looms unsolvable, having a caring authority figure share the worry is a tremendous help. People pay psychiatrists and counselors for the same comfort. I determined that day to be that listener, and never again space out and make my open-door policy a sham.

It occurred to me then that I had been faking it with my department for some time. I had been delegating work to others because of my projects, and that was necessary. But I had also been delegating *me* to others, which cannot be done. I had sent employees to my supervisors or leads, when what they wanted was my ear. I had disrespected their respect for me. Now it was time to regain the trust of my team.

At the next monthly staff meeting I talked to my people about what their definition of open door policy was. I wanted to be clear about my recent actions.

"What does 'open door policy' mean to you?" I asked them, and got several enthusiastic responses. I wrote each answer on a large whiteboard. I faced them and asked for their feedback on whether I was meeting their definitions.

The response was not so enthusiastic. Some gave embarrassed little nods with eyes downcast. I got some frowns and head-shaking, but no one said anything. Not a word.

I could see that their perception of me was negative. I took the lively response to my first question to mean they were eager to reveal their wants, but the silent response to the next question meant I was failing. They did not want to tell me that, maybe because they wanted to spare my feelings. Even so, the blame for their perception lay squarely on my doorstep.

It was time then to start the perception reparation process. I knew I had to be transparent with them. People can tell if you're being evasive. Straight shooters resonate with people seeking answers. I began with an apology. It had to be heartfelt or it would fall flat. Believe me, I meant it.

I thanked them for the much needed wake-up call. I vowed to improve, and asked their help to do the right thing. I said; "Touch my shoulder if I don't turn to greet you when you walk into my office. Or call my name. Wave something. Don't let me off the hook." I asked them to do whatever was necessary to get my attention, because I never wanted them to feel unimportant in my office or my life.

While the apology went a long way, it was ultimately the passage of time and the sustained change of my behavior -- sticking to my word -- that altered their perception of me. I earned back their trust.

Key Actions to building Trust:

1. **Be Transparent:** Tell the truth, not what you think the listener wants to hear. Make no excuses, even if you believe them. Admit mistakes. Allow others to speak with candor, without being upset by their plain words. Encourage candor by responding to negatives with a patient, non-defensive manner. This will invite truth, and cultivate your ability to deal properly with it.

2. **Speak With Sincerity:** Listen carefully. Pay attention to body language and respond positively.
3. **Recognize Your Faults:** We all have them. If you are angered by someone else's failing, you will have no patience with your own. Others will feel relief if you acknowledge your imperfection. It removes the burden of self-condemnation from your people and fosters openness. They will come to you at the start of a pinch, before it snowballs into a catastrophe. You will be seen as "real."
4. **Make a Commitment to Change:** Changes can be small and they can be gradual. However, once you recognize in yourself something that negatively affects your team, commit to making a change. If you learn that morning

greetings are thrown your way and you ignore them, commit to making a change. Have your people agree to be louder or more conspicuous visually. Do not dismiss the concern. You may still fail to hear them later on, but they recognize your effort. They will internalize your regard for them in taking them seriously. That always yields good results, whether in an employee or a relative, or a friend.

5. **Follow Through**: Once you have made a commitment, you *must* follow through. If you fail to remedy the challenge, be transparent. Admit your mistake and resolve to try again. Make notes for yourself. Impress on your mind the necessity to follow through.

Once you have established a strong bond of trust with your team, you will realize the benefits. When people know they can count on your word, they commit to you. They will eagerly work to exceed your expectations, both out of gratitude and for the opportunity to get praise from you. There is no cynicism in acknowledging this truth. Salesmen count on this sort of bond of obligation. It's why they have praise for you. Unlike the cynical salesman, you're not trying to get some selfish hook into a fish. Instead, you're bonding with your employee, treating him as you want to be treated. That's a tremendous upside for them. Take your upside gladly.

Patience

My husband and I home school the four youngest children. Patience is a required subject in our little university. The children are required to exhibit it, as well as we teachers. We tell the little darlings, "If you run out of patience, it's because you never had it in the first place."

I used to call myself lucky for having to be patient with homeschooling; it taught me patience at work. It is true that patience grows stronger with use. But the strength required by patience is akin to the strength required to step out of the way of a falling anvil. It should be effortless. If you want to stay and take the hit, your motivation is wrong.

Impatience is a sign of cruelty. The act of driving a car is not cruel, but willfully driving it over someone when you can take the trouble to stop or swerve, certainly is. An employee --let's call him John -- came to my office a lot in a small space of time. He complained of business and personal problems. Each time I listened and we discussed solutions. My work began to pile up like overripe fruit, as I dealt with John and other leadership challenges.

His visits were taking too much of my time, as well eating up his own work time. Clearly, I had to let him know this, but I didn't want to make him feel unwelcome, or lose his trust. When he next came in I belabored him with a five-minute diatribe about the extreme pressures of my priority projects. I could see in his expression that he was taking this personally. John took my benignly delivered screed as an accusation. I was accusing him of wasting my time. It wasn't my intent, just as the driver fixing her makeup or searching for a cd has no intention of running over the pedestrian. I spoke without considering the reaction to my words, from John's point of view. It was a moment of cruelty, and I was wrong.

It was necessary to give the talk to John. By tailoring my words to suit his orientation, I would be like the driver who watched the road, avoiding accidents. John's reaction caused me to focus better, and I saw that I was wrong. The message was fine; the delivery was not. I immediately apologized. I explained why I was sorry, and set up a time later when we could talk.

You can run out of air, or energy or strength. But patience is a state of being. It's a bottomless well of love that decimates its emotional foes, all with the ease of simply stepping out of the way. You won't step out of the way if you don't see what's falling on you, so stay alert. Stay conscious of the moment. If you feel overwhelmed, as I did with my deadline project, all the more reason to take a breath.

What sparks anger is a feeling of lack of control. So, stop trying to control people or events. You will influence them by virtue of what you do and say, and who you are. If your influence fails to change people or circumstances, look at the facts. Maybe you can try different actions or words. Go ahead and try, try again; all without the slightest shred of impatience, because impatience deters your people from trusting you. It breaks the precious bond so vital to a team. Breaking the bond can be like puncturing a tire. You may not see it deflate for a long time. By then you may be stuck without assistance when you need your mobility the most.

Key Actions to Achieving Patience

1. **Always live in the Moment:** By living in the moment, you put the past away. You see and hear the now. Now matters. The issues weighing on you are better handled at the proper time, with the proper focus. Write down what you have to do and post it where you will see it. There, now you won't forget. Your mind is free to deal with

the present, so do so. Don't worry over the future, or what took place in the past. Don't worry. Worry boosts stress and that's not good for your health. By living in the moment, you give yourself freedom. You can focus then on what is important, without prejudice and without emotional baggage.
2. **Practice Self-Control:** Emotional reactions happen when you lose self-control. Here is an exercise that should help you practice self-control. Do this exercise daily.
    a. **At the beginning of your day analyze yourself and identify areas where you lose control (what triggers an emotional reaction in you).**

b. **Throughout the day practice restraint in those areas**
c. **At the end of your day, analyze your results:** During this final analysis of the day simply recognize where you lost control. See where you maintained control, and mentally note to work harder in areas where you slipped. Do not berate yourself or hang on to any negative thoughts, but simply see what triggered the event. You can resist reacting incorrectly when the same situation arises again. Do not let guilt feelings arise, because they muddy the water of understanding.

3. **Step Back From Stress:** Stress! It's your unwelcome cousin Bradley wedging his way through the door, to raid the fridge and drop crumbs everywhere. He doesn't come empty-handed. He presents boxes of nervous tension and cartons of worry, with a bottle of guilt he insists you uncork right away. But instead of reciprocating with the expected negative emotional responses, maintain control. As the pressure mounts, disengage. You can step back from events without shutting down like a popped fuse. Let the situation unfold without your trying to stop it. Pretend you are watching a movie, so that you follow what's happening without needing to control it. Your control will be over yourself and your

emotions. You will find great satisfaction in that. Afterward if you are alone, close your eyes and allow your thoughts to fall away. When you are still and quiet in this fashion, you may find your center, and peace and calm will flow through you. After regrouping, you can address what would have bothered you. Without disturbing thoughts and welling emotions, you can use your good sense and knowledge to plan a solution.

Once you have achieved patience, others will remark about how calm they feel in your presence. Your presence alone will bring peace to those around you and this will create a secure environment for your team. That security will translate into a strong committed team.

Note: Because I had broken John's trust by laying a guilt trip on him for using up my time, I worked to repair our relationship. I am happy to report he forgave the breach, and we got on well after that. He took less of my time after this. He might have done the same had I treated him with more respect. But all's well that ends well.

By developing a bond of trust with your team and living through patience, you create a loving environment. Your team feels secure and openness comes easy to them.

Chapter 2

Show Sympathy, be Empathetic

Compassion is the father, and sympathy and empathy are his well-behaved children. These twin feelings are both related to caring toward others, but they are not quite identical.

With sympathy you feel for a person. You may not fully understand what they are going through, but you make allowances for them based on their troubles.

Empathy on the other hand requires you to put yourself in the place of other people and share their feelings. Sympathy can be dry. Lose someone close to you, and complete strangers will say they are sorry for your loss. Sympathy is little more than recognition of someone's trials. But empathy is a plumper emotion. Empathy can develop into a bond of deeper understanding which more effectively assuages someone's pain. Alcoholics Anonymous brings alcoholics together, precisely because they can empathize with one another.

The idea of empathy implies a much more active process than sympathy does. It takes work for you to be empathetic to a person's feelings but it can be easy for you to feel sympathy.

Sympathy can leave someone feeling alone. Empathy on the other hand suggests you are right there with him.

Sympathy serves its purpose. As an initial reaction to any of the myriad miseries that occurs in our lives, sympathy has a vital role. Immediately bursting into tears at bad news will not work. Once you have had a chance to digest the information, then you can move to empathy.

I have been privy to more sorrowful happenings than I care to remember. One incident that stands out happened to an employee who worked for me more than ten years, let's call her Olympia. We were close, and I counted her as a friend. In the wee hours one morning the phone woke me, and she wailed, "They killed my baby!" That shocked me out of my sleep stupor.

Olympia had five sons. One of her boys was graduating high school, and at a celebration party, some crashers started a fight. Olympia's son saw his friend in trouble and went to his aid. He was stabbed in the heart, and died immediately.

My initial reaction to her call was sympathy. The standard blandishments came to mind, and I spoke them mechanically. I said I'm there for you, and told her to call on me for anything she needs, et cetera. I did the best I could at 3am.

After the call, I sent emails to the executives of our company, and to friends. Olympia's grief was soaking in, and I segued from sympathy to deep empathy. Empathy for Olympia impelled me to ease things for her as much as possible. I became immersed in her grief. There were arrangements for the funeral to be made. Her family had to carry on with their lives. I gladly helped where I could. Sympathy created the promise; empathy spurred the action. I cried with Olympia and she shared stories of her baby boy. Although I had not lost a son, I have two, and could imagine the universe of grief the murder of one of them would give me.

Empathy for your employee, or for anyone for that matter, gives you the perspective you need to take the right decisions, based on compassion. Olympia had no vacation or sick time available, so I arranged to have her peers donate some of their time off, so that in addition to her standard bereavement leave, she could have a protracted leave of absence without losing income. She still had four boys to support.

Here is an employee who will always be loyal. Of course, I did not act out of selfish design, but treating people with compassion has reciprocal blessings. Olympia would move mountains to help me if I asked her to. Gratitude is human nature.

Key Actions to Showing Sympathy

1. **Respond with concern:** Acknowledge the situation and offer words of sympathy such as: "I am sorry for your loss" or "It must be difficult for you"
2. **Offer your shoulder, or ear:** Let him know that you are available to listen to him
3. **Offer to help:** Ask if there is anything you can do for him.

Key Actions to Being Empathetic

Practice Empathy: Practice using empathy the next time you're in a situation where someone is suffering emotionally.

1. Be with him and listen
2. Don't talk just to say something. Be still and the right words will come at the right time
3. Let him express his feelings, wait to share yours
4. As you listen, begin to put yourself in his situation
5. Don't try to fix the situation, just be near him with your heart open to him

6. When you are moved to respond, do so and let him know that you understand

Use sympathy when you are in a situation that requires a quick response of acknowledgement of an employee's situation. Showing sympathy in a crisis versus reacting in a harsh uncaring manner is an act of kindness.

Use empathy. You will be a better leader for it. You will be known for your understanding and compassion.

Through empathy, you communicate genuinely, gain a better understanding of someone, improve cooperation, and create an environment of trust, respect, and excellence.

Chapter 3

Emotional Stability

In order to be a compassionate leader, you must understand emotional impacts and you *must* possess emotional stability.

Emotional stability allows you to understand your own feelings while being able to perceive the feelings of others. Emotional stability enables you to motivate others, and protect and manage all relationships.

The key elements to emotional stability are understanding intent versus impact, understanding your emotional triggers, and recognizing when you have triggered others. Also, it is knowing what to do about emotions that are ignited by those triggers.

There are two sides to every issue. While you can only have ownership of your side of the conversation, you can influence the outcome by how you handle your end, using emotional stability to impact positively the other half of the dialogue.

Intent vs. Impact

Intent is the result you expect from your words or actions. The impact is the actual result, expected or not. Before speaking, know how the listener will take it. You may call a pretty woman "phat," but first ensure she will know which phat you speak of. Consider the true impact of what you say and do, not the impact you believe you should get. Good intentions do not count.

Good intentions once had a surprising impact after a company "all hands meeting," that everyone attended. One of my supervisors, "Terry," stood up thanked his team for all their recent hard work and overtime. He named each of them and gave them certificates of appreciation. He also gave each a $50.00 gift card. His intention was wonderful: give his team recognition and motivate them to continue working hard. The meeting was at the end of the day, and the impact was clear in the morning.

I got dozens of complaints. They sent emails and left voicemails about Terry's decision to reward his people. Employees from other teams were unhappy they had not received similar treatment. Other supervisors complained they had not been given the option to reward their teams. Still others complained that Terry's team did not deserve recognition, that their work was substandard. Some said Terry was overworking his team, and they were agitated and impatient.

The president of the division left me a long, gaseous voice message demanding to know why this team was singled out for kudos when everyone across the company was putting in extra time and effort.

I talked to Terry about intent versus impact. I explained that singling out his team made his people feel good, but it alienated others. He had not considered any negative impact from a goodwill gesture, and asked how he could have foreseen such a brouhaha.

I had an answer for Terry.

Steps to considering potential impacts:

1. Know your audience:
   a. Terry knew the employees were highly competitive. Also, jealous. A pizza party for team A had to snowball into similar feasts for teams B through Z or there would be trouble. When everybody was burning the overtime oil, they would recoil at just one team being thanked.
2. Terry might have considered that other supervisors would seem chintzy

and ungrateful in light of his generosity.
3. Talk to others:
   a. If Terry had checked with me, his boss, or even bounced the idea off a peer, he may have been warned. Together, we could coordinate some sort of formal thanks for the reps. Alone, he stirred up a hornet's nest.

You can't catch every possible impact but taking time to consider others before you take action, can help to reduce surprises. It is no fun to move forward with good intentions, only to discover negative impacts.

Here's a negative impact on a smaller, personal scale. When she was in high school, my eldest daughter Katie had an overweight friend, "Sandy." Sandy asked Katie to sort of coach her on losing weight, in fact she asked Katie to nag her aggressively. At a school dance, Sandy was letting too many snack table goodies go chuckling merrily down her gullet. Dutifully, Katie told her that she should cool it on the snacks. Shockingly, Sandy started crying, and loudly decried Katie's "cruelty." She made quite the scene, embarrassing herself and Katie tremendously.

Katie felt just terrible. Her intent was good. Her intervention was requested, for Pete's sake. She was confused, and when she came to me I asked if she had warned Sandy off the snacks in front of others. Katie had indeed chided Sandy where friends could not help but hear. Mystery solved, yet my daughter got defensive when I pinpointed this faux pas. She retorted that, after all, Sandy had asked for it. She was emphatic about her own good intention. So, how could she have known?

I had an answer for Katie.

More steps to considering potential impacts:

1. Put yourself in their shoes: Katie had been scolded in public before. By me, in fact. And one time her father punished her by making her do pushups at a crowded park. She

was mortified each time; she should have drawn on these experiences to put Sandy's request in context. She was not asking for humiliation, but encouragement. As I reminded Katie of this and asked her to put herself in Sandy's place, she understood completely.
2. Play out the scenario in your head: Katie could have played out the scene in her head. She might have realized how embarrassing it would be to speak out, and could have delivered her message *sotto voce.* Whisper next time, I told her.

If your well-intentioned words or actions negatively affected others, speak to those you have impacted. The conversation can be difficult but the key to leading with compassion lies in the ability to speak truth while preserving relationships. It is precisely during difficult exchanges that you will encourage openness and honesty, or else alienate somebody. Close the gap between your intent and your impact, and remember to apologize. It won't cost much, and sincere apologies rarely backfire.

Some mindsets make difficult conversations *more* difficult. It is important to avoid using these mindsets.

Mindsets to avoid when engaging in difficult conversations:

1. **Right and Wrong:** Remember there are two sides to each story. Enter into the conversation with an open mind.

2. **Intent and Impact:** We cannot know for sure what someone else's motives are, and our own can be misunderstood. Be ready to concede that there was an unexpected impact, and go directly to creating the correct and positive impact.

3. **Blame:** Avoid pointing fingers at anyone, including yourself. Assigning blame is not necessary. Stay focused on the prize, which is getting to the proper impact of your initial intent. Listen, talk, share, but keep blame in the vault.

Emotional Triggers

Emotional triggers are words or actions that spark an emotional response. Anyone can cause an emotional response, but it takes a special person to mitigate its affect.

Tools to use when your emotional trigger is pressed:

1. **Recognize it:** If you are having an emotional reaction, your body temperature may rise, your mouth may get dry, and your skin may feel overly sensitive or prickly. Perhaps you will feel the pulse in your temples, get a headache, or feel blood rush to your face. You may feel anger or sadness, self-pity or embarrassment. You may feel a

combo of negative effects. This type of stress will make you very sick eventually, and can even lead to death. It's why high-pressure businessmen turn up their toes early in life. Bottom line -- recognize when these negative reactions hit, so you can eliminate them and keep ownership of you. Later, I will suggest an exercise that has helped me to achieve greater self-awareness and self-control.

2. **Create Space:** Once you see you have been triggered emotionally, mentally separate yourself from your thoughts. Breathe deeply, maybe take a good stretch. The idea is to deflect your stream of emotions, to let them pass. Stand back from them. Do not try to

suppress them or hold them in, because this will make you blow a gasket sooner or later. Think of your emotions as a river. You do not need to jump in, but let it flow by. Anger may come, but do not accept it and it will not dominate you. It will seem as though you are eavesdropping on someone else's anger.
3. **Respond:** Responding to an emotionally charged situation can be touchy. When emotions run high, relationships teeter on a very shaky ledge. There are a few different ways to respond which can help keep the relationship in balance. In some cases, you may want to *respond with openness and honesty.* Let the other person know that he has affected you. Be

polite. Start with a phrase as direct as, "When you said such-and such it made me feel…" Or "That remark is hurtful. What is your intention by using those words?" Asking someone his intent is an extremely tactful way to remind the other person that he has been insensitive. Being open and honest and encouraging others to do so helps to create a safe, comfortable environment for your team. Another way to respond is to *ignore the faux pas in the moment and address it later when emotions are in check.* At times, you may be too volatile to address the emotional sting in the moment. Or you may recognize that the other person is too volatile. Either way, if addressing it in the moment will make the situation worse, let it pass and address it later. When you go back to discuss the offense be sure to do so calmly and be honest. Do not chicken out or forget to resolve this issue. It isn't fair to you or to the other person. If he really does not know he offended you, he is likely to commit the same offense again. By courageously addressing the situation, you build a stronger relationship with the other person, and being informed will help him in his other relationships as well.

Another alternative is to ignore it altogether – let it go. What set you off -- words or actions -- may not be so objectionable. If there is no clear problem here, do not create one. Make sure you do not suppress your anger to let it build up for later explosion -- let it go. Let it go. Let it go. It bears repeating.

One afternoon I was visited by another manager who had an issue with me. To be kind, let's call her Medusa. Medusa stalked into my office and barreled at me with her claws describing an exaggerated square that terminated a scant inch from my nose. She bit off each sarcastic word through tightened jaws. "I ... need you ... to think ... outside ... the box!"
Flashbulbs popped. Nails scraped slate. Glaciers imploded. Razors rasped on bone. With my adrenaline rush I could have levitated and made her head explode

with my mind. It seemed that I was having a severe emotional reaction. I had been triggered, and had to get control back or else give in to some vicious emotions. Prison beckoned.

First, I moved my chair back. That returned my personal bubble to me.

Deep breath, exhale, relax, then let rage do its dirty little dance without any buy-in from me.

"I can see that this is important to you," I said brightly. "Now what is it specifically I can do for you?"

Kazoos whaaaahed. Shutters closed. Balloons deflated. Fish resumed swimming in their bowls. My ingenuous answer and unemotional reaction to Medusa shifted the event from the confrontation she was ready for, to an opportunity to help us both. On one hand,

I got the chance to practice patience and understanding, while on the other hand Medusa got the chance to see somebody behave the way she should behave -- as an adult. Her anger was stymied. What else could she do now but explain herself? I listened to her problem and helped her with a solution. Then, when she was calm, I addressed her rudeness. And she apologized.

As I mentioned earlier, I have an exercise designed to help you recognize when you are emotionally triggered.

Building Strategy for Recognizing Emotional Triggers

Recall a memory within the last 2 weeks of an experience you had that fits the following criteria:

- You felt dissatisfied with yourself in a interaction and you had strong feelings about another person who was involved in the situation

- You experienced a sense of discomfort during and after the occurrence

- As you recall this occurrence, now you have the same sense of discomfort

On a piece of paper, answer the following questions about this memory:

1. Describe the situation in 2-3 sentences.
2. What was the dominant feeling that you experienced?
3. How are you feeling now as you recall this event?
4. If you are alone, recall the memory aloud in front of a mirror.
5. As you repeat this event in front of the mirror, observe your body language, tone of voice, speed and volume, etc.
6. When you have finished, write down your observations.

If you can practice this exercise with a partner, use the following:

Speaker's Instructions:

- Tell Your partner the responses you listed for questions 1-3

- Notice how you felt discussing this with your partner

Listener's Instructions:

- Listen to what your partner is telling you. You may paraphrase or check your understanding of what is being said if needed

- Observe your partner's body language, tone of voice, speed and volume as he is speaking about this event

- When your partner is finished speaking, ask: "How did it make you feel to say this to me?"

- Tell your partner what you observed as he spoke

The things that you observed about yourself or that your partner observed about you are indicators of how you respond when you are emotionally triggered. These observations will help you to recognize, in the moment, when you have been emotionally triggered. I would suggest that you repeat this exercise several times over the course of weeks or months. The more you do this, the more self-aware you will become.

Tools to use if you have pressed the emotional trigger of another:

Leading With Compassion

Recognize it: It is important to pay attention to tone and body language while conversing. If the other person folds his arms or frowns, shakes his head, raises his voice or disengages from the conversation, you probably said or did something to trigger this reaction. Negative impacts manifest in many ways. Observing people's reactions is a skill that will improve with practice.

Address it:

- **Bracket:** Before you address your perceptions, step back from your emotions and proceed in a calm, non-defensive manner.
- **Check perceptions:** Mention your observation and ask if you are correct. If someone says you

misread him, he's fine with it, great. If he is not okay, and you did emotionally derail him, take ownership of the mistake and go on.
- **Apologize:** It is always okay to say "I'm sorry."

One afternoon during a meeting, one of the managers--let's call her Sarah--would not let go of an issue she felt strongly about. Like a broken record, she kept repeating herself over and over again. Frustrated, I said, "I think we have gone over that issue more than once. We really need to keep on track in order address all of the agenda items." Sarah was offended. She crossed her arms at her chest and stopped talking altogether. Clearly, I had triggered a negative emotional response. Sarah disengaged from the discussion and I decided to reengage her. I apologized. Sarah seemed surprised and relieved that I brought it out in the open. She accepted my apology and we got our meeting back on track.

Addressing issues in the moment can feel awkward at first and the words might seem insincere. It takes practice. If you make mistakes as you begin this process, it's okay. Give yourself time. You will improve. Applying emotional stability means engaging in difficult conversations, and being open to addressing the emotional triggers you or someone else falls prey to. The crucial element of this leadership is compassion. With compassion and strength to execute these difficult tasks you will achieve a respected leadership that all will bring success as surely as the rain and sun cause flowers to grow and bloom.

Chapter 4

A Little Kindness Goes a Long Way

Kindness is the calm, gentle caring we give each other. It is giving without expectation of anything in return. Kindness is a virtue.

When I was a cute and irresistible little girl, my grandma used to say that it costs nothing to give a compliment. She told me do it often, but cautioned me only to compliment when it is deserved. She said it would change people for the better. I could not understand at the time, but I bought the idea that it was good to praise the deserving. One afternoon my grandmother was watching me vacuum our house, and when I was finished she said, "Wow, you are really good at maneuvering that vacuum cleaner." I recall I had been in a bad mood while I was doing chores, but after Grandma complimented me on a job well done, I felt great. I felt special. I was in a good mood. I was only 10 years old at the time but I never forgot the impact of that compliment. Sometimes a kind word is all it takes to make someone's day. You can make a positive impact on people with a little kindness, and what does it cost? You can afford it!

Principles of Kindness in Leadership:

1. **Kindness generates positive energy:** The waves that you generate when you offer kindness toward another, has a ripple effect that can be far reaching.

2. **Kindness should come from within and be automatic:** If you are not easy with kind gestures and find difficulty being sincere, you must practice. Grant simple acts of kindness every day. Kindness will become second nature. Simple acts are as simple as smiling,

sharing a laugh, offering small compliments. If someone looks nice, say so. Say hello with a smile in your voice as well as on your face, to each person on your team. When a stranger walks into the office, greet him with a smile and a give a warm handshake, with both hands. Make him feel welcome. At a store, greet the person at the checkout counter with a smile. Ask him how he's doing. You may notice lots of smiles generated by simple acts of kindness. A smile is contagious.

Eventually all these calculated, simple acts of kindness will translate into a change in you. You will want to be kind to others. You will listen closer to what others say, which will make you perceptibly engaged. People will believe in you, and you will believe in yourself.

3. **Rudeness and cruelty generate negative energy:** Just as kindness generates waves of positive energy, rudeness and cruelty generate waves of negative energy.

4. **Kindness is not a sign of weakness, but of strength:** If someone is rude to you, is it easier to be angry or to respond with kindness? The usual response is anger, and most make the mistake of thinking this is the natural, acceptable reaction. "I'm only human." Yet, anger is an animal response. Humanity is marked by reason. It takes reason, and strength of character to give kindness in response to rudeness.

I have often heard women speakers preach that for a woman to show kindness reveals her to be weak. According to them women must be firm, strong, and logical, but never soft and kind. They are absolutely wrong. First because the qualities they endorse are not nullified by kindness. In difficult encounters the power comes in being right. If you have you have to steamroll over the opposition to your ideas, maybe your ideas are lacking. Avoiding a difficult conversation by reprimanding someone in a one-sided discussion gives you the momentum. You put the other side on their guard, but you also alienate your audience. Bullying is not leadership, and giving others the chance to speak doesn't vitiate your authority. You will be appreciated for your forbearance in letting others have their say.

Both men and women *need* to show kindness in the workplace. The world is a hard, cold place, and the business world is even harder and colder. Kindness to others brings in a warmth many will appreciate very much. That appreciation will bring the dedication and commitment of your staff. They will be loyal to you.

5. **Role Model Appropriate Behaviors:** Once you become a leader, people will watch you. They will emulate your behaviors. Your integrity must be consistently demonstrated.

A few years ago, I had a young woman who worked for me who recently had been promoted to a leadership role. I noticed that when she walked the floor her head was down and her expression was grim. When someone asked her a question, she rarely looked them in the eye. I heard complaints from her staff about having to work for her. Her demeanor intimidated them. They found her cold and unengaged.

I met with her about this. She had no clue they felt this way about her. I had her try an experiment for two weeks, where every time she crossed the floor she held her head high and smiled, meeting the eyes of her people. I told her to say hello, and to respond to questions with eye contact and warmth in her voice.

After two weeks she was excited about the improvement in her relationship with her staff. By smiling and acknowledging others, she connected to her people, and she could feel the change in how they felt about her. By showing a little interest in them (simple acts of kindness), she had brought her staff together to form a close team. Over time, she became one of the best managers I ever had the pleasure to work with. She had gone from a shy, disengaged figurehead to a kind, compassionate leader.

True success in leadership requires being kind. Kindness generates positive emotions in others and evokes a sense of well-being. As a leader, you will benefit from your kindness. You will get more out of your employees because they see you give more of yourself to them.

When my husband Gerald was an army infantryman, he banged his shin and developed Cellulitis in his leg. He was put on light duty by the doctor, and was given crutches. He found that when he was up and active he did not need the crutches, but after sitting for a while he did, because his leg was extremely painful until walking got the blood flowing again.

His platoon sergeant saw him enter the mess hall on his own two feet, carrying his crutches. After eating, he needed the crutches. The sergeant confronted Gerald in front of many of his fellow soldiers, accusing him of being a "shamdog," or someone who is faking hurt to get out of duty.

Gerald told the sergeant about the way the pain came and went, but the man refused to believe. He told Gerald that as far as he was concerned, he was a "goldbricker." After this, my husband felt self-conscious whenever he needed the crutches.

A couple of days later the sergeant needed a replacement in the field for something very important to him. He asked Gerald to ignore his light duty profile, and consent to going into the field, as a personal favor to the sergeant. Ever the plain talker, Gerald told his sergeant that he would be glad to go the extra mile, to take the pain and help out, except for the fact he had a bad leader. He told the sergeant that by condemning him as a liar when he didn't know what he was talking about, he de-motivated him. He would not do the sergeant the favor.

This demonstrates the problem with unkind, uncompassionate leadership. Of course your employees sign up to work, but often you may wish to ask something more of them. Perhaps you ask them to do overtime, or work extra hard to reach a goal. If you never are willing to go the extra mile for them, why should they wish to do so for you? Yet give them more of yourself, treat them with kindness and compassion, and most will jump at the chance to help you in return.

Conclusion: Compassion Breeds Commitment

When you are a compassionate leader you give a little of yourself to each person on your team, and to everyone around you. The positive energy that you generate spreads throughout the workplace.

The key elements to being a compassionate leader are displaying love, sympathy, empathy, emotional stability and kindness. Your leadership should be marked with sincerity. Grudging compassion is no virtue. Kindness not freely given will not reap the benefits of true kindness.

As a compassionate leader, I never expected anything in return for my leadership. Yet I always have had staff bending over backwards to help me, not just in business but in daily life.

As a compassionate leader, you may have to get used to accepting graciously gifts from grateful employees. Do not refuse the gifts unless they go against your employers' rules --- they are given with love, and why should anyone refuse love? As a leader, you have a lot of people to look after, so you will not be expected to give gifts in return, *quid pro quo.* Be gracious and thankful, and return the love. You deserve the loyalty and favor of your staff, so be happy. You earned it.

One indicator of the impact a compassionate leader makes, is how many former employees stay in touch. I am in touch still with dozens of people who used to work for me. We communicate by phone or by computer. Facebook has made everyone easy to find if they wish to be found.

I hope this book makes an impact on some leaders. It requires commitment, because results may be too long in coming for some. Others may find it more expedient to promotion to be the Captain Bligh of the workplace. You will know if your desire to lead with compassion is successful, when you are told by your people that they never had a leader as good as you. The downside to this is that when you move on, you leave a lot of sad people behind. This is why we need many more compassionate leaders.

ABOUT THE AUTHOR

Katherine Parks has been in the business world for more than 25 years. She started in the file room and moved her way up the ranks through various management positions. She has managed teams of people ranging in size from as little as 12 people to as large as 400.

She has won awards from the companies she has worked for which describe her as a leader. In 2010, she won the We Care and Give Back Inspiration Award while working for Intuit.

She is married, has six children and lives in Stockton, California. She and Gerald homeschool their four youngest children. She is currently writing and teaching others how to lead with compassion.

www.ingramcontent.com/pod-product-compliance
Lightning Source LLC
Chambersburg PA
CBHW071733040426
42446CB00012B/2346